To Tomorrow's Young Inventors,
I hope these adventures spark your curiosity and
inspire you to transform the world
through science and inventions!
-Praba & Pumpus

To Mom, Dad, Ramani, & Abhi,
Your support and inspiration has allowed me to
share my passion for inventing with others
and bring Pumpus to life.
Thank you!
-Praba

praba@boon-dah.com
www.boon-dah.com

Ordering Information:
Quantity sales. Special discounts are available on quantity purchases by corporations, associations, and others. For details, contact the publisher at the e-mail above.

Publisher's Cataloging-in-Publication Data
provided by Five Rainbows Cataloging Services

Names: Praba, author.
Title: Pumpus has a growing idea! / by Praba.
Description: Tampa, FL : BOON-dah, 2019. | Summary: Pumpus and his pals must use his book of ideas and inventions to solve a water problem. | Grades Pre-K to 4.
Identifiers: LCCN 2019904824 | ISBN 978-1-7330059-0-6 (hardcover) | ISBN 978-1-7330059-1-3 (paperback) | ISBN 978-1-7330059-2-0 (ebook)
Subjects: LCSH: Picture books for children. | CYAC: Gardening--Fiction. | Water--Fiction. | Inventions--Fiction. | Science projects--Fiction. | Friendship--Fiction. | BISAC: JUVENILE FICTION / Science & Nature / General. | JUVENILE FICTION / Technology / Inventions. | JUVENILE FICTION / Social Themes / Friendship.

Classification: LCC PZ7.1.P73 Pu 2019 (print) | LCC PZ7.1.P73 (ebook) | DDC [E]--dc23.

Pumpus Has a Growing Idea!

by Praba

Illustrated by Heather Forde,
cover art based on the work of Jack Spellman

Boon-dah Books
Tampa, FL

Pumpus loved to read about great ideas and inventions. His favorite inventors were Grace Hopper and Thomas Edison.

Pumpus had two best friends,
Filbin and Filberta,
who loved to hang out with him,
especially when he went on gardening
adventures.

It was a beautiful spring morning.
Pumpus and his friends were planning to plant their
vegetable garden on a patch of land they had
found in the woods that also had a
well and a water tap.

They started their hike early and reached the spot.

They were all ready to begin the fun gardening activities they had planned, but as Pumpus checked the well and turned on the water tap, he suddenly realized something...

...the tap had very little water coming out.

"Oh, no!" said Filbin and Filberta,
and they wondered if the fun they had
planned for the day
would be a distant dream.

Luckily, Pumpus had brought his book of inventions, where he kept the best ideas of his favorite inventors.

"Boon-dah!" Pumpus yelled.
"I have an idea! Let's make our own
trickler-sprinkler," said Pumpus.

"What is a trickler-sprinkler?"
asked the puzzled Filbin.

"It says here in my book of inventions that a trickler-sprinkler is a way of applying water *slowly* to the roots of plants," explained Pumpus.

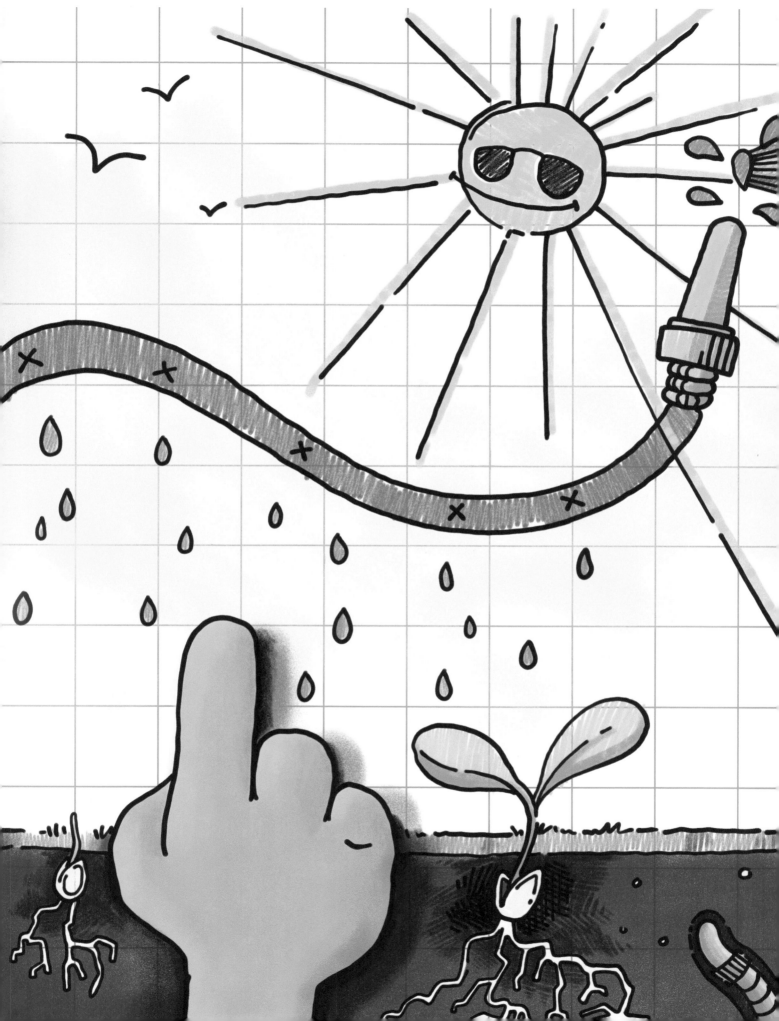

"How do you apply water slowly to the roots?"
asked Filberta.

"By using pipes that have very tiny holes in them,"
explained Pumpus.
He showed his friends the long hose he had in his toolbox.
Filbin and Filberta grew excited!

Pumpus quickly extended the hose and
gathered the tools he would need in order to build a
trickler-sprinkler model, also known as a prototype.
He was careful to follow all the safety rules
and to wear gardening gloves.

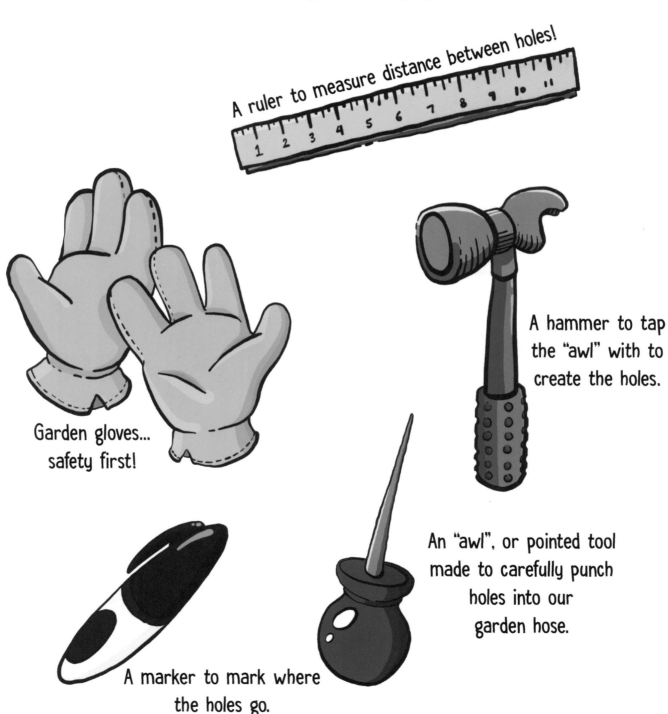

A ruler to measure distance between holes!

Garden gloves...
safety first!

A hammer to tap
the "awl" with to
create the holes.

An "awl", or pointed tool
made to carefully punch
holes into our
garden hose.

A marker to mark where
the holes go.

Pumpus made tiny holes along the hose
-one every twelve inches-
and was ready to place the hose in the ground.
Suddenly, he realized...

...they didn't have any mulch!
"Uh, oh!" said Filberta and Filbin, worried that the plants
wouldn't grow if they couldn't keep the ground moist.
But then, something happened.

Pumpus quickly realized that the dried leaves
in the forest, which were still on the ground
from last fall, were similar to mulch.

Filbin and Filberta quickly gathered lots of dried leaves
while Pumpus started placing the plants.
The friends worked together until the dried leaves were
placed around each plant.

"The leaves will help keep the soil around the roots moist as the water drips from the hose," Pumpus explained. "And that's how a trickler-sprinkler works."

Before turning the tap on, Pumpus connected one end of the hose to the water tap and then sealed the other end to avoid any water leaks.

After three months, Pumpus and his friends
returned to the garden, and Boon-dah!

There were beautiful, tall plants, where they had planted them,
and best of all, they had lots of vegetables!
"Hooray!" said Filbin and Filberta in amazement.
They gave Pumpus a big hug.

That night, the three friends shared stories about their outdoor adventures, came up with ideas on how they could help protect the earth, and snacked on the vegetables from their garden.

It was the best gardening adventure ever!

For Parents & Teachers

What is a "Trickler-Sprinkler"?

Irrigation is a process of applying controlled amounts of water to plants at needed intervals. Farmers around the world use irrigation systems to water their crops, because rainfall alone is not enough to help grow their plants. A trickler-sprinkler is a form of irrigation, where water is brought directly to the root zone of the plants via pipes with small holes drilled in, spaced equally apart. Since almost no water is lost through evaporation, the soil has plenty of opportunity to absorb and hold water for plants. Also called "drip irrigation", a trickler-sprinkler is used when water is scarce, and was developed by Simcha Blass, a Polish-Israeli engineer and inventor, with his son, Yeshayahu.

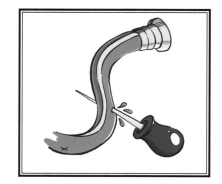

Make your own Trickler-Sprinkler

CAUTION: Always take the help of an adult

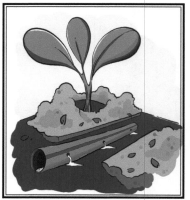

You will need:
Old garden hoses
Mulch or dry leaves
Ice pick or awl
Marker Pen
Gardening gloves

Procedure:
1. Dig a 5-inch deep trench close to the plants.
2. Pull both ends of the hose to straighten it.
3. Using a marker pen, mark the hose every 12 inches where each plant or seedling is growing.
4. Ask your parent or an adult to poke a hole in the hose at each mark using an ice pick or awl.
5. Cap the end of the hose that is not connected to the tap.
6. Place the hose down into the trench, along each row, and cover with mulch or dry leaves.
7. Cover the mulch or dry leaves at the top with soil.
8. Gently turn on the tap enough to fill the hose to the end, making sure not to overfill the hose, or it will result in a full sprinkler system.
9. Let the water run on low for around 8 hours.
10. Check to find out how far the water has penetrated the soil.
11. Accordingly adjust the water pressure.
12. Take note on the time required to water your garden entirely.

Garden Safety For Kids

-Always do gardening with your parents or adults.

-Use thick rubber gloves and wash them after you are done with gardening.

-Always let your parents or adults use sharp tools.

-Do not touch or use any chemicals such as weed killers or fertilizers.

-Never eat any plant, flower, berry, seed, nut or mushroom found in or on the ground.

-Mushrooms can spring up overnight, and many toxic mushrooms look like ones that are good to eat. Pick up and throw away mushrooms right away to avoid dangerous mistakes.

-If you have a pet, check with your veterinarian for a list of plants that can be poisonous for them.

-Leave chemicals, like insecticides, fertilizers and weed killers, in their original package, and NEVER move chemicals to an empty food or drink container or package.

-To check if a plant is toxic, bring a clipping to your local nursery for identification, or call your local poison control center for a list of local poisonous plants.

-Keep the phone number for your poison control center posted in your house, garage, or anywhere you keep chemicals. If someone might have been exposed to a poison, call right away. Fast expert help is available 24 hours a day, seven days a week.

1-800-222-1222

Glossary

Boon-dah: *interjection* | boon·dah | \ bün·dä \
Used as an exclamation to express triumph upon a discovery or invention. Also used as an exclamation to express an idea to solve a problem.
Example: Thomas Edison had a boon-dah moment when he invented the right filament for his light bulb.

Inch: noun | \ 'inch\
A unit of linear measure equal to one twelfth of a foot
(12 inches = 1 foot). |——— one inch ———|

Prototype: noun | pro·to·type | \'\prō-te-tīp\
The first full-scale, and usually functional, form of a new type or design of a construction (such as an airplane)

Further Reading...

Drip Irrigation:
Gardening With Less Water, David A. Bainbridge
(2015, Storey Publishing)

Grace Hopper:
Grace Hopper: Queen of Computer Code,
Laurie Wallmark (2017, Sterling Children's Books)

Thomas Edison:
Who Was Thomas Alva Edison?,
Margaret Frith (2005, Penguin Workshop)

Sign up to receive
Pumpusville Times
at www.boon-dah.com
and learn more about all the books
coming soon in the STEAM series.
Scan the QR Code below for
direct access to the website,
where you can meet Pumpus!

CPSIA information can be obtained
at www.ICGtesting.com
Printed in the USA
BVHW021133040919
557500BV00003B/13/P